UEA SCRIPTWRITING 2016

UNIVERSITY OF EAST ANGLIA
CREATIVE WRITING MA
SCRIPTWRITING
ANTHOLOGY
2016

FOREWORD

TIMBERLAKE
WERTENBAKER

THE UEA's MA SCRIPTWRITING Anthology
brings together the work of the 2015/2016 new MA course
in scriptwriting, led by Steve Waters. There's been intense
work, reading, watching films, discussion, writing and
rewriting, all in a very supportive and non prescriptive
environment, which is so important for writers. The
students have been able to test their work in front of
their peers and have had the advantage of Steve's wisdom
and experience as he is himself one of our best and most
interesting playwrights.

Plays need not only to be written and seen: they also
need to be published. This is very important and allows
them to be thrown into the future. I often imagine someone, someday, even many generations from now, browsing
through published texts and suddenly finding the one play
that speaks to him, to her. The calibre of the writers I met
on this course makes it more than possible that one of these
will be in this book.

Timberlake Wertenbaker
Professor of Playwriting

INTRODUCTION

STEVE WATERS

IT'S A PLEASURE TO WRITE the introduction
to this year's Script anthology, for the first cohort of
students I have taken through their MA as convenor. As
ever, each offers a portal into their author's world, each
has their own taste and concerns, filtered through personal
memory and private imagination. Yet there is a shared
public energy to the work which I hope has emerged out
of the vigorous conversation we have had amongst
ourselves: encounters and stand-offs, challenges and
dares drive these short works.

What's striking is the strong flavour of place and
time here. Sometimes it's the savour of the immediate
present: so Patrick Hughes gives us a disturbingly funny
sense of how growing up on the internet might lead to a
new relationship with strangers in 'Letter to Vikki', whilst
Eleanor Herzog crafts a haunting monologue of loss and
ambivalence ('Written in the Sky, Buried in the Ground'),
her subtle meditation on the shooting down of a plane
over Ukraine. However Jonathan Cross takes us back
to an earlier trauma, imagining the reality only touched
on in Elizabeth Bishop's seminal poem 'In the Waiting
Room' and gives it a 'local habitation and a name'. Whilst
Andreas Hadjivassiliou characteristically defies definition
and category replacing them with urgency and wit in
'Cake', Simon Farnham allows the war on all our minds to
crash in on his table-turning head to head 'Heraclea'. The
past returns in 'Emanate', John Ingram's exuberant and
spooky account of a childhood epiphany in an Irish suburb,
while Keith Bradley serves up LOLs in 'Keeping Up with
Joneses', his tenderly observed account of '80s Manchester.
Finally in 'Beached' James McDermott brings us right up
to date with a gloves-off account of growing up gay
in Norfolk.

It's no small matter to travel so far so fast; the
short play or film offers 'no hiding place' as Jonathan
Franzen once said of the short story. But that also creates

possibilities arising from the challenge of travelling light, unburdened by the heavy luggage of exposition. What's also gratifying here is the variety of form itself – from solo play to tense duologue, from short wordless film to salty verbal comedy, from absurdism to naturalism to the post-dramatic and back. I've seen all of these pieces emerge in classes and workshops, but they are now independent entities, speed dates with the imagination – I hope you enjoy the journey.

Steve Waters, *convenor of the*
MA in Creative Writing: Script

KEITH BRADLEY

KEEPING UP WITH
THE JONESES

ACT ONE
SCENE ONE

A Monday evening in 1979.

A split stage. In the centre the Bradshaws' living room. The wallpaper is of a floral design and badly nicotine-stained at the top. There is a gas fire, a mantelpiece covered in brass knick-knacks, an old sofa and two armchairs .The television (out of view from the audience) is switched on but the sound is low. The distinctive voice of Margaret Thatcher and a Panorama-*style news reader can occasionally be heard.*

An exit stage left from the living room to a hall. There are some hooks on the wall with a few coats on them. Stairs lead to the upstairs rooms.

An exit stage right to a small kitchen with a sink, some cupboards, a fridge and a cooker with a chip pan on it.

> SUSAN, *mid 50s, and* SALLY, *her sister, a good ten years younger, are seated in the armchairs side by side looking through a mail order catalogue. Susan looks up at the television.*

*

SUSAN: I suppose we're going to get *her* all week now. Politicians, they're all the same. Just out for themselves.

SALLY: Still at least it's a woman this time.

SUSAN: David doesn't trust her.

SALLY: She can't be any worse than that last one.

SUSAN: I'll turn it off till *Blankety Blank*'s on.
> *She gets up and turns the television off.*

SALLY: Now come on, our Susan, look at these (*indicating the catalogue*). You've got to get with it, times are changing. People are more open-minded these days. More adventurous.

SUSAN: Are you saying I'm narrow-minded?

SALLY: No, not at all, but it's just that your, well, your living room looks like you, well, the furniture looks like you bought it in 1950.

SUSAN: We *did* buy it in 1950. Me and our mother. You were in a pram. We pushed you in a pram all the way down Alexandra Road. You never stopped skriking. We were thrilled to bits with the furniture then.

SALLY: I know, but it is very old and out of date now.

PAUSE

SUSAN: I suppose it isn't that much when you pay it over thirty-eight weeks at ninety-five pence a week is it? What does that work out at?

SALLY: Oh I don't know but it must be less than forty pounds and you deserve a new sofa. Go on treat yourself.

SUSAN: Sofa?

SALLY: It's what they call them these days. They're not settees anymore, they're sofas. I think it's French.

SUSAN: Well, I suppose I – are you sure it's less than forty pounds?

SALLY: *Yes* I'm sure. I'm certain it is.

SUSAN: You don't sound sure. We can ask our Michael when he gets in. (*She looks at the clock*). Oh I can't wait till he gets home. He said he thought they had tea at seven.

SALLY: (*Putting her hand on* SUSAN*'s knee*). The Joneses call it dinner. *PAUSE*. Dinner. And listen. They have (*slowly enunciating each word separately*) the – vegetables – on – the – table. On the table.

SUSAN: (*confused*) What do you mean they have the vegetables on the table?

SALLY: Maggie Yates told me. Her Dennis, Michael's friend, went round there for tea, I mean dinner, once. They put all the vegetables in a big serving dish on the table and you help yourself *at the table*.

SUSAN (*still confused*): At the table?

SALLY: Yes, rather than putting the vegetables on the plate

in the kitchen and then bringing the plates to the table
with the vegetables on, they bring the plates to the table
with no vegetables.

> *This is the most incredible thing* SUSAN *has
> ever heard.*

SUSAN: So the plates are on the table with *no* vegetables
on?

SALLY: Yes. Exactly!

SUSAN: I've heard some strange things in my time but that
really is odd. I mean, why *would* you want to do that?

SALLY: I think it's so you can just take as many as you want.

SUSAN: Still, it's a bit a odd.

> PAUSE

SALLY: Now what about a nice set of cushions to go with
your new sofa?

SUSAN (*enthusiastic*): Oh yes! Definitely, I can't have my
shabby old cushions with new furniture. Our mum
would turn in her grave.

> *The sound of the front door opening.* SALLY *and*
> SUSAN *look in the direction of the hall.* MICHAEL,
> *13, wearing dark eye shadow and pale skin toner à la
> Siouxsie and the Banshees enters. Perhaps he is singing
> the opening verse to* Hong Kong Garden. SALLY *and*
> SUSAN *look at him horrified.*

SUSAN: Oh my God, Michael. You (*slowly enunciating each
word separately*) have – not – been – round – to –
Jocelyn – Jones's – like – *that?*

MICHAEL: Like what?

SUSAN: Like *that?*

MICHAEL: Like *what?*

SUSAN: I can't believe you've shown me up like this and at
the Joneses. Oh my God. What will people think?

> *She gets up and paces the room.* MICHAEL *sits down
> on the sofa.* SALLY *gets up and sits next to* MICHAEL
> *on the sofa.*

SALLY (*soft*): You didn't *really* go to the Joneses dressed like that, did you?

MICHAEL (*angry*): Yes I did, Auntie Sally. I put on make-up, like a popstar. Like plenty of other people.

    LONG PAUSE.

    SALLY *puts her arm around* MICHAEL.

SALLY (*soft*): Now, our Michael, *PAUSE.* We've, your mum and dad and me (*struggles for the words*). We've always told you that you can tell us anything, haven't we?

    Michael shakes himself free.

MICHAEL: What are you talking about?

SALLY: You can tell us anything – we won't mind.

MICHAEL: Aunty Sally, what the hell are you talking about?

SALLY: Well you know *PAUSE* (*at a near total loss for words*), we know you're *artistic*. We understand that. We know you have artistic tastes. But you're not. . . It would break your Uncle Bob's heart.

    SUSAN *sits down.*

SUSAN: Michael, stop acting the goat, you know perfectly well what Aunty Sally means.

MICHAEL: I don't know what any of you mean! Where's Dad? He doesn't get in a tizzy fit worrying about what other people think.

SUSAN: Your dad's on lates this week and he's sleeping. Me and your dad work very hard for you and we just want to be proud of you, that's all. Now, I don't mind you dressing like that in your bedroom but not in other people's houses. I bet Peter Jones doesn't dress like that at home.

MICHAEL: That's exactly how Pete dresses at home. In fact, if you think I'm bad you should take a look at how Pete *does* dress at home. He's twice as bad as me. More make-up and black fingernails.

SALLY: Black fingernails?

MICHAEL: Yes, black fingernails.

SALLY: What? Even at the table?

MICHAEL: Yes, even at the table.

SUSAN: What, while they're getting their vegetables?

MICHAEL (*rapid*): Yeah, even in the house, even at the table, even eating vegetables.

> *A LONG PAUSE.*

SALLY: What's their house like?

MICHAEL: What do you mean "what's it like"?

SALLY: I mean what's it like? Is it clean?

SUSAN: Is Mrs Jones house-proud? Does she clean up?

MICHAEL: I don't know, it's just a house. It's just like ours.

> SALLY *smiles at* SUSAN. *This is news to warm her asprirational heart.*

SALLY: What are the Joneses like?

MICHAEL: What do you mean, what are they like? They're just people like us.

SALLY: So they're no different?

MICHAEL: No.

SALLY: No? Not at all?

MICHAEL: No.

> *A LONG PAUSE.*

SUSAN: Oh come on, our Michael, there must be some differences.

MICHAEL: Well, nobody shouts.

SUSAN (*rapid*): What do you mean, nobody shouts?

MICHAEL: Nobody shouts. When Mr Jones's dinner is ready, Mrs Jones *walks* to his study to tell him.

SUSAN: Nobody shouts here neither.

MICHAEL: Yes they do!

SUSAN: (*turns around and shouts*) DAVID!!!! Come and listen to what your son's saying.

> *From offstage the disgruntled sound of* DAVID BRADSHAW *being woken up.*

DAVID (*off stage*): Bloody hell! What now?

> MICHAEL *stretches his palms out as if to say I rest my case.*

SUSAN: How much is thirty-eight weeks at ninety-five pence a week, our Michael?

The sound of Hong Kong Garden *by Siouxsie and the Banshees.*

BLACKOUT

JONATHAN CROSS

IN THE WAITING ROOM

1. EXT. STREET – DAY
Worcester, Massachusetts – 1918.
ELIZABETH *(6) is being pulled along by her* AUNT *(30s) past huge white tents with nurses working frantically.*
She watches men dig trenches long and deep, narrowly dodging a wagon headed towards her.
She passes a sign reading: Spitting Spreads Spanish Influenza. DON'T SPIT.

2. INT. DENTIST – CONTINUOUS
AUNT *and* ELIZABETH *approach the receptionist's desk; she is wearing an influenza mask.*

> RECEPTIONIST
> Ms Consuela?

> AUNT
> Yes, to see Dr Samuels.

> RECEPTIONIST
> Is this for both of you?

ELIZABETH *looks up at her* AUNT.

> AUNT
> Just me.

3. INT. WAITING ROOM – CONTINUOUS
AUNT *sits* ELIZABETH *down on a chair – sunlight is piercing the waiting room. Dust flies.*

> AUNT
> Show these gentlemen how well behaved you
> are, hmm?

AUNT *goes to leave,* ELIZABETH *follows.*

> ELIZABETH
> I don't want to be alone.

> AUNT
>
> Don't be silly, I won't be long.

*AUNT leaves. ELIZABETH stares back at the MAN nearby,
he turns away.*
*She glances around the room for something to do. MAN
extends a magazine to her, she sees the brown spots on his face.*

> MAN
>
> Do you good to read something. There's
> pictures too.

> ELIZABETH
>
> I don't like reading.

> MAN
>
> Don't be cheeky, young lady.

*She takes the magazine, slumps awkwardly on a chair opposite
and flicks through* National Geographic.
*She ignores the first few pages, clumsily flicks through a hand-
ful more, until a picture of a volcano catches her eye – then
some hikers – then…*
*She sits closer to the light – tribal women. Their elongated
necks catch her eye to start with. She looks down and sees their
breasts, horrified.*
She looks for a date as if it will calm her down – 1918.

> AUNT (OS)
>
> Oh!

*ELIZABETH looks up – tears the picture of the women out
– and runs to her AUNT. MAN tries to intervene but she slips
past him.*

4. INT. DENTIST'S ROOM – CONTINUOUS
*ELIZABETH hurtles through the door – she slows down as if
it hadn't happened. She taps her AUNT on the knee.*

ELIZABETH
Auntie… They scared me too, see –

AUNT *has a magazine clipping of naked women pushed in her face. She sits up, apologises to* DENTIST.

AUNT
Goodness Elizabeth, I was trying to have my teeth inspected. Please go back to the waiting room, your mother will be disappointed to hear this.

The DENTIST *lowers his influenza mask to light up. He calls through –*

DENTIST
Annie?!

RECEPTIONIST *arrives hurriedly.*

DENTIST
I've got enough patients for one day.

DENTIST *signals to* ELIZABETH, RECEPTIONIST *grabs her hand and escorts her back to the waiting room.*

ELIZABETH
I like your name. I thought you had my name. But I like your name more, you should keep that one.

RECEPTIONIST
Thank you. I like your name, too.

As they are about to reach the waiting room, AUNT *snatches* ELIZABETH *away from* RECEPTIONIST.

AUNT
Please can I urge you never to touch a patient. This is common decency.

RECEPTIONIST
Miss, I was only helping her back to her seat.

They argue – unheard by ELIZABETH *– she looks up at them both, giants at war.*
She looks back at the picture of the women – forcibly wiping her face of tears.

5. INT. WAITING ROOM – CONTINUOUS
Unseen, she walks back to the waiting room, putting the picture back in the magazine. She turns to MAN.

> ELIZABETH
> Thanks for the book, mister.

MAN *nods and leans back.* ELIZABETH *heads back to her* AUNT.
Unnoticed by her, MAN *collapses on the floor unconscious.*
NURSES *descend with white sheets and roll his body onto a stretcher.*

END.

SIMON FARNHAM

HERACLEA

ACT TWO

Mix of news soundbites relating to Iraq, Syria etc. Noise fades out and sounds of a face being punched. Lights reveal NAJIB *tied to a chair, face is swollen and bleeding. Sound of a door opening and closing.* ADAM *emerges. He's smoking a cigarette. He walks up behind* NAJIB *and looks down at him. He blows smoke at the back of* NAJIB*'s head.*

*

NAJIB: No more please. (*spits out blood*).
> *Adam finishes his cigarette and undoes the handcuffs behind the chair and cuts the ropes holding* NAJIB*'s ankles.* NAJIB *slumps forward.* ADAM *catches him and lifts him from the chair.*

NAJIB: (*groans*)

ADAM: Come on mate.
> *They shuffle to a door and into a rubble-strewn alleyway.* ADAM *rests* NAJIB *down against the wall and sits opposite.* NAJIB *looks up and shields his eyes.*

ADAM: That's daylight, Najib.

NAJIB: How d'you know my name?

ADAM: From your passport.

NAJIB: Oh. (*looks up the sky again, squints and looks back down shielding his eyes*)

ADAM: How long's it been since you saw it last? Daylight, I mean.

NAJIB: (*touches wounds on face*) Don't know. Couple of weeks maybe?

ADAM: Just one week. Time flies when you're having fun. They normally don't last this long?

NAJIB: What?

ADAM: Daesh the Kurds capture. Interrogation. Confession. Execution. Four, five days max.

NAJIB: So why ain't I dead?

ADAM: Have a guess.

NAJIB: I don't know.

ADAM: It's me, Naj. I'm keeping you alive.

NAJIB: What?

ADAM: Me, Naj. Right now I'm the best friend you've got coz I'm working my nuts off to keep you breathing. No one from the UK even knows you're here except me. And there's no Geneva Convention here.

NAJIB: No what?

ADAM: Funny, didn't think you'd be working within the rules.

NAJIB: About what?

ADAM: Forget it.

> NAJIB *continues to touch his wounds.*

NAJIB: You got any water?

> ADAM *pulls a bottle of water from a map pocket.*

ADAM: Here.

> *Throws it into* NAJIB's *lap.* NAJIB *drinks then recoils with pain.*

ADAM: Teeth a bit sensitive?

> NAJIB *drinks from the bottle.*

It's OK Naj, you don't have to thank me?

NAJIB: Uh?

ADAM: You know, for the water and keeping you alive.

NAJIB: No one asked you to. Why d'you do it?

ADAM: Because I think you've been taken advantage of. Because I recognise you Najib Sather of 48, Inkerman Road. I've seen you grow up. Running round the streets with your mates, playing cricket on the corner, throwing stones at drunk people walking home from the pub. So that's why I'm stepping in, to try and save your life because it's something that might actually be worth saving in amongst all this shit.

NAJIB: What you mean?

ADAM: That I don't buy all that shit about no choices.

There's always choices.

NAJIB: Oh yeah, like what? I ain't got no GCSEs. Even my brother won't give me a job.

ADAM: What, at the takeaway?

NAJIB: Yeah.

ADAM: Why not?

NAJIB: Forget it.

ADAM: No Naj, why not?

NAJIB: Says I ain't smart enough. That I can't even drive.

ADAM: He's wrong Naj. You're smart enough to work for him, but right now you need to work with me. Shit Naj, don't you recognise me from around the neighbourhood?

NAJIB: Nah.

ADAM: Fucking hell, kids. Always staring at the floor. As you walk along the street of life, you look up more the older you get.

NAJIB: What the fuck?

ADAM: Nothing, it's just something a mate of mine said once. Anyway Naj, you need to start looking up as it were, because you're in shit street and right now I'm your only fucking hope.

NAJIB: How you gonna save me?

ADAM: I've struck a bargain with them Naj, and to be fair, it's not the best in the world but it'll keep you alive. Like I said, all you have to do is work with me.

NAJIB: What I gotta do?

ADAM: Fess up Naj.

NAJIB: What?

ADAM: Confess. Confess to all the shit you've done while you've been with them.

NAJIB: Shit man, I've told them everything I know. They don't tell us much so we can't tell anyone if we get caught. A week I've been in that room. Beatings, electric, shitting myself, and I can't say anymore coz I don't know anymore.

NAJIB *starts sobbing. Adam watches. Sounds of jet aircraft.* ADAM *looks up.*

ADAM: Well, they've got what they needed in that respect.

NAJIB: Eh?

ADAM: How do you think those planes know where to go? They're taking out the targets you identified. You're fucked now, Naj. You can't go back. You know what they'll do to you for talking. For people who don't like art they seem quite creative when it comes to killing. (*pause*) Look, all you have to do to stay alive is to say a little bit more.

NAJIB: I don't know no more.

ADAM: That's not the point.

NAJIB: What d'you mean?

ADAM: They want you to confess to murders, tortures, rapes and stuff that you were involved in. They'll film it, bang it on YouTube, hand you over to the SAS or whoever and you get dragged off and tried for murder somewhere.

NAJIB: Where?

ADAM: I don't know Naj but it won't be here. That's all you need to be concerned about. It'll probably be the UK. If it is you'll be fine. You'll do easy time getting protected by the gangs inside. Piece of piss. Read the Koran, maybe learn a trade, get out, start a new life. It doesn't matter Naj. As long as you're out of here you're alive. There's probably even some fucking human rights lawyer who'll win you a load of money. Nice little nest egg for when you get out. Alternatively you can have your nuts cut off by Kurdish women soldiers who'll stand around laughing as you bleed to death. Your choice boy.

NAJ *looks down at the floor. He throws some small bits of concrete around.*

NAJIB: You know it wasn't just about doing bad shit man.

ADAM: What wasn't?

NAJIB: Leaving home and coming out here.

ADAM: No?

NAJIB: No.

ADAM: What else was it about then?

NAJIB: It's about you lot.

ADAM: Us lot?

NAJIB: Yeah, you, the West, your governments and foreign policy and stuff. Bombing the fuck out of Palestine, Libya, Iraq, Afghanistan. Us Muslims gotta stick together man, otherwise you'll bomb us all. It's like the Crusades.

ADAM: Really Naj? Is it? So the Kurds, the Yazidis, anyone who doesn't represent your own fucking twisted brand of Islam is fair game right? This isn't about doing the right thing. This is about a few rich and powerful men spreading Wahhabism so they can be more powerful. Yes, the West fucked Iraq and Libya with little thought given to what was going on before, during or after, but what IS are doing isn't about revenge, it's about using religion as an excuse to exploit the vacuum created by all that. And fuck it Naj, I don't think you're even all that religious. You're just using it as an excuse for a bit of adventure. An adventure that's gone wrong because it's not how you imagined. So all you've got to do is just talk about the bad stuff and get the fuck out of here because, trust me, you're dead if you don't.

    NAJIB *plays with concrete again.*

NAJIB: Nah, fuck it man, you're just…

ADAM: Naj, those women will be here in less than an hour so you've got to start fucking listening to me. Just confess to your crimes, get the fuck out of here, and try and get your life back together again at some point. You're out your fucking depth here and you know it.

NAJIB: What? In an hour? They can't do that. No man.

    NAJIB *tries to stand but falls back down.*

ADAM: Fucking yes, man. In less than an hour they're

going to cut your cock and bollocks off, stab you in the arse and stand around laughing and filming it on their phones as you writhe around in agony at their feet.

NAJIB: No man, not me. This can't be fucking happening.

ADAM: Yes Naj, yes you, yes it is happening. Now start talking, anything, tell me anything so I can at least buy you some time.

NAJIB: Like what?

ADAM: Like anything. Anything bad. Anything that will stop them killing you and making your brother think he was right about you. He would never dream of coming out here. Even if he did, he wouldn't get caught. That's what he'll be thinking when he finds out, he'll be saying…

NAJIB: Shut up man, you don't talk about my family.

ADAM: Then talk for fuck's sake.

NAJIB: What do you want me to say?

ADAM: Just the bad stuff. What have you done to people here that's proper bad?

    NAJIB *draws in the dust with a stick.*

NAJIB: There was some girls.

ADAM: Girls? What girls? Where?

NAJIB: I don't know, a few weeks back, in some town.

ADAM: And what happened Naj?

NAJIB: They gave them to us.

ADAM: Who, who did?

NAJIB: The men in charge.

ADAM: How many of them were there, Naj?

NAJIB: About six I think.

ADAM: How old were they Naj?

NAJIB: I dunno, maybe ten, maybe twelve.

ADAM: Who were they Naj?

NAJIB: Christians, Yazidis.

ADAM: How many of you were there Naj?

NAJIB: I dunno.

ADAM: A hundred, two hundred?

NAJIB: Maybe a hundred.

ADAM: And what did you do to them, Naj?

NAJIB: We fucked them.

ADAM: What, all of you?

NAJIB: Yeah, I guess…

ADAM: You raped them, the little girls, you raped them
    didn't you, Naj?

NAJIB: Yeah, I guess…

ADAM: And what did you do after Naj? What did you do
    after all one hundred of you had gang-raped those six
    little girls?

NAJIB: We…

ADAM: You what?

NAJIB: We covered them in petrol and set them on fire.

ADAM: And what did you all do while they were burning to
    death Naj?

NAJIB: We…

ADAM: You what Naj?

NAJIB: We laughed.

ADAM: You laughed.

        NAJIB *sobs.* ADAM *pats* NAJIB *on the back.*

ADAM: There you go, Naj. That wasn't so bad Naj was it?
    Well done.

NAJIB: What now? Do I have to tell the camera?

ADAM: No need Naj, look.

        ADAM *points up. A hand is holding a video camera*
        out of a window.

ADAM: You get all that?

        Hand gives a thumbs up signal.

NAJIB: So what now?

ADAM: It's over Naj.

NAJIB: So when do I go?

        ADAM *pulls an automatic pistol and points it against*
        NAJIB's *head.*

ADAM: You don't Naj, you're going nowhere. It's over.

NAJIB: But you said… No please, no man, no please, no,

not like this. Not here. Please.

    ADAM *handcuffs* NAJIB *to a drainpipe.*

ADAM: You don't get off that easily, boy.

    ADAM *puts his pistol back in its holster and lights*
    a cigarette.

ADAM: OK, I'm off. See you in a bit.

NAJIB: What? Where you going?

ADAM: Me? I'm off to get some petrol so you go out in
flames. In the meantime, there's some Kurdish women
who'd like to meet you. Enjoy paradise Naj, I hear
it's great.

    ADAM *walks off down the alleyway. Lights to black.*
    Sounds of footsteps over rubble. NAJIB *starts*
    screaming.

ANDREAS HADJIVASSILIOU

CAKE

SKY *and* MARLA *sit cross-legged, almost facing each other;*
slanted a little towards the audience.
SKY *has a gun in one hand and a single bullet in the other.*

*

SKY: We have options.

MARLA: Hit me.

SKY: The first is we just sit here.

MARLA: Yeah. Relax.

SKY: No, not relax. Sit here till someone comes or till we
    die.

MARLA: Doesn't mean we can't relax.

SKY: Think I'd struggle.

MARLA: Fine. What's two?

SKY: Two is I shoot you.

MARLA: Nah. Three?

SKY: Three is you shoot me.

MARLA: How would you feel about that?

SKY: Not great.

MARLA: None of these options are great.

SKY: I'd feel extra not great about that one.

MARLA: What's the point in two and three?

SKY: Quicker end.

MARLA: And sustenance for the other I guess.

SKY: That's disgusting.

MARLA: We're entirely detached from polite society. We
    don't need to obey etiquette.

SKY: Not eating someone doesn't fall under etiquette.

MARLA: It's unspoken etiquette.

    PAUSE.

SKY: I'm removing option three from the table. There is no
    option three.

MARLA: So the choice is whether I want to get shot or not?

SKY: Yes.

MARLA: I don't.

SKY: All right. New option three –

MARLA: You said it was off the table.

SKY: Old option three is off the table. This is new option three. Option three 2.0.

MARLA: Hit me.

SKY: We line up our heads and we shoot both of us in one.

MARLA: Hm.

SKY: No?

MARLA: I don't want the last thing that goes through my head to be some of yours.

SKY: We don't have to do it that way round.

MARLA: I also don't want to get shot.

SKY: Fine. Well I don't just want to sit here.

MARLA: Old option three would help.

SKY: It's vetoed.

MARLA: Well we need another option then.

SKY: I gave you one.

MARLA: Well we need another other option then.

      PAUSE.

SKY: All right. Let's deal with this like the last piece of cake.

MARLA: Eat it?

SKY: No. Didn't you do the last piece of cake thing?

MARLA: What last piece of cake thing?

SKY: What did your family do if there was only one piece of cake left?

MARLA: Someone would go, 'Can I have the last piece of cake?' and everyone else would go 'Yes' and then they'd eat it.

SKY: Christ.

MARLA: What?

SKY: No one wants to be the one who takes the last thing of a thing.

MARLA: I do.

SKY: Then you're a barbarian.

MARLA: Fine. How do *you* deal with the last piece of cake?

SKY: Everyone notices that there's only one piece of cake

left. Then someone says, 'Does anyone want the last piece of cake?' And everyone says 'God no' but they're probably lying and everyone else knows it. So we turn off the light. And then whoever wants it just takes it, free from social judgement.

    PAUSE.

MARLA: Why would you do that?

SKY: 'Cause it's impolite to take the last piece.

MARLA: It's impolite to lie. I think it's one of the ten commandments.

SKY: It's not.

MARLA: So what are you on about? What's the option?

SKY: Option four. I put the bullet in the gun.

    (*She does so*)

And I put the gun here.

    (*She puts the gun between them*)

And we close our eyes.

    (*Neither do*)

Close your eyes.

    They close their eyes.

MARLA: And now?

SKY: We wait until someone decides they want the last piece of cake.

MARLA: All right.

    She takes a deep breath.
    So does Sky.
    They sit, silent, eyes closed.

ELEANOR HERZOG

WRITTEN IN THE SKY,
BURIED IN THE GROUND

DRAMATIS PERSONA:

JEL, *a thirty-year-old English woman.*

SETTING:

A chair on stage facing the audience with a single light on it.
The rest of the stage is in darkness.

*

JEL walks on stage, envelope in hand, sits down.
JEL: I'm not the type of person to get involved with
sentimental stuff like a time capsule. No. Not for me.
They kept saying bring something important to help us
connect with the future but who's interested in what I've
got to say? What have I got to leave behind?
JEL holds up letter briefly.
But then this fell through my letterbox so I thought, well,
there's something.
I mean, it doesn't mean a thing to me so the best thing for it
is just get them to bury it in the ground.
JEL looks at the letter for a moment.
When they shot that plane clean out the sky, I didn't give it a
thought. No. Because it's been another year full of the usual
news grinding up against everything else.
If it's like this for me now I can't imagine what it's like for
you but it's like bang, there goes another little corner of the
heart you have to surround with police tape. Another date
scorched into the grey matter. And there's so many now it's
hard to pick out the bits that are important.
And I didn't think a plane shot down over Ukraine meant
that much, really.
To me. Here. Now.
And even when I got the letter I only worked out he was one
of the ones because the stamp wasn't from where he said
he'd be. Was going. I thought that couldn't be the stopover
and even if it were why'd he post it from some borderland?
JEL looks at the letter for a longer moment.

His handwriting on the envelope so I reckon that what
happened was whoever was looting the wreckage must
have found it in his pocket next to his passport. All sealed
and ready to send. So who knows why but they must have
stuck a few stamps on it and popped it into the post office.
Or whatever it's called out there.

> JEL *takes the letter out of the envelope and opens it
> briefly before refolding and running her nail over
> the crease.*

And yeah, it is a love letter.
Which is fine because I didn't love him. It would have been
worse if I'd loved him.

> *PAUSE.*

They're nice words and everything but look, I just couldn't
get over how he'd wander around the house without a top
on and his gut out.
Around my house.
Like he thought he was some Adonis and –
I shouldn't say this but I don't think anyone is vetting so
I will. When I fucked him, he used to do this thing where
he'd growl like a dog. I'd nearly be there and he'd start
growling and I'd be too busy trying to work out what kind
of dog he sounded like that when he finished, I wouldn't
know whether to laugh or cry.
But my God that Italian cooking.
I'd wake up and he'd have gone out and got fresh everything
from the market to make this low-fat fry-up. Eggs with
parmesan and baked tomatoes and we'd just sit there taking
our time. Having coffee after coffee and just taking
our time.

> JEL *leans down and puts the letter on the floor by
> her feet.*

It's me that went up to him the first time we met. He was
sat there, reading a paper in this dingy, old pub. Not sure if
you know the type now but like one that never pulled itself
out of Victorian London and neither did the lady serving

drinks. I'd just popped in to get out the sleet and he didn't
even look at me when I sat down, just kind of shuffled his
things along the bar. I had to ask what the news was before
he looked up.

I took him home that night.

I didn't even mind the growling that first time.

God, do you ever feel like when you're with someone and it
feels like it might be – like it might be something really –
I don't know.

But later all it is is just a smear on your bed sheets. And all
you remember is a body. Flesh and blood and maybe your
hands holding onto it but –

I didn't even take him to meet my family. I just couldn't.
There'd be so much watching and judging and checking
he had the same table manners. He wanted to though.
Thought he should come for Christmas otherwise he'd be
on his own. I told him no. I just couldn't bear him hanging
on my arm the whole time and speaking to anyone who
would listen. Writers are like that, you know. Put a couple
of drinks in them and they'll spin out some anecdote they
think reverberates with your innermost being or grind you
down with questions like they have some God-given right
to know your very soul.

> JEL *picks up the letter, scrunches is slightly in
> her hand.*

Anyway. It was like that movie, *Life Is Beautiful.* Or maybe
it's more like *Sliding Doors.* Only it's like when you get
stuck on the tube and the doors won't open and the person
sat next to you elbows you every time they turn the page.
That's what our relationship was like.

And that's not a good place to be, is it?

I told him that, too, with his breakfasts and his pecorino
and his kissing in public places. I told him not to.

Spitalfields we'd go. Brick Lane too. I like to try on vintage
dresses and eat bad curry and he didn't seem to mind
coming along. But it was like he'd come on the condition

he could hold my hand and if I said anything he'd go all
quiet and pretend to be fascinated by recycled pocket
watches until he forgot about it and tried to hold my hand
again. Drove me crazy. And they're bringing back his
body this Sunday.

Then they're sending it on to Italy so I won't see hi –
I won't see the coffin or anything. That's just for his mum
and a dad. Probably a Nonna too but I never asked. It's f
unny to think of them all the way over there and grieving
and they never knew me. Never knew all the things we did.

    PAUSE.

They say that it all goes before your eyes. Everything. All
those moments. Even those you forgot. I'm not sure I'd like
that. Reckon we forget so we can protect ourselves. Get on
in life. Not dwell. But I reckon it would be like that moment,
you know, like when you feel like there's something bigger
than you. Like on fireworks night when you smell the
gunpowder and think of your dad and Catherine wheels.
Or… or maybe like when you listen to *The Shipping
Forecast* and hate it but you still fall down on your knees
and sob. Maybe that's how he felt as he fell through the sky.

    PAUSE.

My friends liked him though. They kept saying he was good
for me. Really good for me. Even when he proposed they
said I should say yes. I didn't though, I didn't love –
I didn't love him.

I didn't want to give up my whole life just because he
was nice and would have been a great dad and was really
excited.

He kept coming up with all these names. Didn't seem to
understand that you can't call a kid Maximilian. So I only
told him afterwards. But… he would just have wanted it
and then where would I have been? Maximilian in one arm,
him grabbing the other and a packet of soggy chips holding
us together.

And when I said goodbye to him he held my body. He held

my body so tight and I could feel his tears running down my cheeks. And it was like I had no air left inside he was holding me so tight. And just as he was nearly gone, I did tell him I'd miss him. Even though I didn't love him, I told him I would miss him. That's how I know it's all OK, you see. Because I told him that. That I'd miss him. So it's OK.

PAUSE.

So I'm leaving you his letter. It's no good to me, just a few words. But it might mean something to you. Whenever they dredge this up.

> JEL *puts the letter back on the floor. She pushes it*
> *forwards with her foot. She nods a few times, stands,*
> *walks off stage.*

PATRICK HUGHES

LETTERS TO VIKKI

PERFORMER

> Back In The USSR *by The Beatles plays. After 30*
> *seconds the track fades.*

This is the voice of Paul McCartney singing *Back In
The USSR* with The Beatles. Released in 1968 and off
The White Album. When I was ten years old this was my
favourite song and The Beatles were quickly becoming my
favourite band. So I did what all fans do in a pre-Internet
era. I decided to write a letter.

> *Reading from a letter taken from the Performer's*
> *pocket.*

"Dear Paul McCartney. My name is Patrick Hughes. I am
ten years old and I love The Beatles. *Back in the USSR* is my
favourite song of all time. My address is on the back of the
letter. I am going to Wales next week so please reply first
class so you don't miss me.

Your biggest fan.

Patrick"

My Mum always used to say to me, aim for the stars and
you might just hit the trees, and that's what I did. I aimed
for the star. I aimed for the scouse son of Liverpool. I
waited by the front door excited for my reply. The holiday
to Wales came and went with nothing. After a few weeks
of sulking I tried again. This time I took my dad's advice,
Patrick, forget about the stars, forget about the trees, just
try and get off the bloody ground son. So I tried again. This
time I set my sights a little lower.

> *Reading from another letter.*

"Dear George Harrison

My name is Patrick Hughes. I am ten years old. I hope you
don't mind if I call you George. I love your music. Keep up
the good work and do some more tracks with Paul. I look
forward to hearing back from you.

Patrick."

Once again I waited. I waited for weeks and still nothing.
I was gutted. At the height of my misery I wrote one more

letter, a couple of sentences to, and I can't believe I'm saying
this, Ringo Starr. Forget the trees and forget the ground,
for me writing to Ringo was like going six feet under. I was
admitting defeat. He was a rubbish drummer and an even
worse scouser but I wrote it. I am ashamed to say I did.

   Reading from another letter.

"Dear Ringo.
My five-year-old brother likes your song *Yellow Submarine*.
Yours,
Patrick"

Well time passes, as we all know it does. Life goes by.
Bills and bank statements come and go. Not much really
happens does it? Well actually, tell a lie, a few years on and
I break my leg. I'm in Spain listening to Paul McCartney's
underrated solo album from 1997 *Flaming Pie* when I slip
on a wet tile and fall through a window. It was a major fuck-
up. My mum has a breakdown, my dad starts smoking and
my two brothers decide that they will never go on another
family holiday again. After a week in a Spanish hospital
I get put in a wheelchair and sent home.

Now, the problem with doing something like that at the
start of the summer means that you miss out on all the fun.
Literally everything. Leg in a cast. Sat in a chair twenty-four
seven. The days and weeks drag. You get lonely. Like really
lonely. I spent hours each day alone in my room.

   *Yesterday by The Beatles plays for 30 seconds. The
   Performer sings along. After that it fades.*

Yesterday. Released in 1965. A perfectly haunting ballad
written by Paul that summed it all up. I felt forgotten. I
felt like I was ten years old again, sat by the letterbox. My
brothers were at football camps and my parents had booked
a coach holiday to Leamington Spa to avoid simultaneous
breakdowns. I was alone. So each day I would do really
menial tasks just to pass the time. I craved attention.
I needed contact and then something happened.
I was organising my spam folder, basically just deleting

emails about Viagra, when I saw it. An email addressed to
me. Addressed to Patrick Hughes. From Vikki Hughes…
Time for a brief family history. I am a Hughes. I have always
been a Hughes. My grandfather was a gamekeeper in
Ireland. He shot birds and deer and planted stuff and had a
great time in the woods. He had a son, my dad, who had my
two brothers and me. That was that. Our family is small.
The Hughes clan is compact and easy to memorise. So,
when I get a message from Vikki Hughes addressed to me,
I'm understandably confused. However, after a bit of email
scanning, it's clear that she's made a mistake. Her son was
another Patrick and she had got his email wrong. He was
travelling around Africa so she was keeping in touch with
emails. Emails to my account. And that is where the story
should end, right? That is where the sane person emails
back explaining the situation: I am not the person that you
are contacting, thank you, sorry and goodbye. That is what
you should do right? Well it didn't go like that.

> She's Leaving Home *by The Beatles plays for 30
> seconds. The Performer mimes conducting the music.
> It fades.*

She's Leaving Home. Written by Paul McCartney. Released
in 1967 from the album *St Pepper's.* In the song Paul talks
about a young girl who leaves home. She leaves a letter,
finally confessing to her family about how she feels. She
knows they will never understand. That letter. The note she
hoped would say more. The power of it. The importance.
This is the song I am listening to as I read the email from
Vikki. The email that I should have deleted. The email that
still sits in my inbox. The email that reads:
"Hi Patrick,
Vikki here. Your mum. I thought I would send you an email
to see how you are doing? How is the travelling? This might
be a silly question but is it hot in Africa? If so, make sure
you are using sun cream.
Love from Dad, Jean, Milly and Wheezy.

Email back if you can."

By this stage I had been stuck inside for nearly a month.
The sun blazed outside. I put a black sheet over my curtains
and I decided, fuck it. I was going to write a reply. I began
to type.

"Dear Mum

Thank you for the email. Just arrived in an Internet café in
Africa. You're right it is hot here. It's a sticky humid heat
but I'm enjoying myself. Please tell me more about what you
are up to. How is the weather back home?

Your son.

Patrick."

I had nailed it. I was proud of my work. I was happy with
it and honestly I thought that would be that... until...
something happened... she replied:

"The weather is still very mild here. Milly is having her
operation next week so fingers crossed. Just got back from
Rome didn't we? It was really lovely."

And I type back:

"I am in Ghana at the moment. Lovely country and lovely
people. Tell me about Rome. I'm moving to Liberia next
week."

Then bing, a reply. Longer, more vivid:

"We stayed in a hotel by the station. I took fifty pictures.
Trigger-happy. We ate in a little restaurant every evening.
I shared a room with Judith. She snores because of her
thyroid operation, so I had to get my earplugs out. Tell me
more, honey.

PS Liberia? I thought you were just travelling around South
Africa?"

Shit. I had to elaborate. I could feel myself slipping deeper
and deeper into the lie but it felt good.

"Dear Mum,

South Africa was dull so I moved west. I have met a lot of
new people and have been trying lots of new food. I ate
a beetle in Senegal and in Mali I saw the national football

team play. It was wonderful. I hope Dad is well. I think about you every day. I will try my best to reply to you as soon as possible. How is Milly?"

Each day Vikki wrote back and I replied. The time flew by. In each email I would describe my surroundings. I started researching West Africa and going into the politics, the cuisine and even throwing in a bit of language at the end of my letters. I kept it vague but still personal. She told me that she missed me. She told me that she loved me. She hung on my every word and I… I got a little carried away. I began to express concern that the politics of Liberia were starting to get a little hairy. In one letter I described an incident on a sandy beach where five men with machetes chased me and my friends into the sea. I told her that incidents like this were frequent here but I was being careful. She was worried. One night she wrote to me in a real state. Milly's operation hadn't gone to plan. The thrombosis in her right foot was bad and she was going to have to have her leg removed. As far as I could tell Milly was my grandmother and she was really sick. I got another email:

"Patrick

Please get back to me as soon as you can. Things are really tough right now and the family needs you. Milly doesn't have long. Is there any way you can make it home? It sounds dangerous where you are. I hope you are safe. Milly asks for you constantly.

Get back to us ASAP.

Please."

She needed me. They needed me, and this was my time to act, but just like Paul and the gang, I didn't reply. I started to feel bad, like really bad… but my leg started to get better. I could now leave the house. So I did.

And in my most cowardly act in my seventeen years on the planet I deleted my email address. I killed the Patrick Hughes who wasn't really me and who definitely wasn't him. He was gone and I was ashamed…. Well, at first I was,

but writing the emails had made me more confident. Like
Patrick, I travelled round the world when I finished school.
Like him I lived my life and I never looked back. Like him
I saw the world. Like him I lived.

So, last week I needed to open a bank account with my
girlfriend. I had to have proof of address from the last ten
years. It was nice to go back home. Rooting through an
old box of young person's bank statements and savings
accounts that had been hurriedly shoved away by my dad,
I found an unopened letter.

>   *The Performer takes out one final letter from*
>   *a pocket.*

Dated 1999, when I was ten years old, addressed to Master
Patrick Hughes. It smelt like dust. The seam opened in my
hand.

"Dear Patrick"

I was overcome with anticipation. My hand trembled as
I read the handwritten note. To me. I looked at the words
and I read.

"Thank you for you letter. I am glad you are a fan. All the
best.

Yours faithfully

Ringo Starr."

And you know what? I didn't feel disappointed or cheated.
I still don't. No. Because at that very moment I couldn't
help think of the real Patrick and all of the gang at home,
together, flicking through pictures of Africa and Rome.
Milly looking down from wherever she is, Wheezy doing
whatever Wheezy did and Dad and Vikki sat there with
broad smiles. Happy again to be with their son…

>   Day Tripper *by The Beatles plays.*

You see it may come as a surprise to you but I actually
learnt something. I learnt that in life… when you reach
out to someone special, someone really important…
sometimes… the reply you get… is not always what
you expect.

JOHN INGRAM

EMANATE

FADE IN:

EXT. GARDEN – DAY

Halloween, 1956: Sun sets over a suburban Dublin cul-de-sac and its enormous, ancient trees.

High in his tree-hut in a Monterey Cypress, REX *(13) – with a dream of empire – is installing a catapult rack.*

OC Sound of fireworks in distance.

EXT. GRAVEYARD – DAY

Door of old, ivy-clad church is locked with large key.

Empty hearse leaves graveyard, stops.

DRIVER *(40) – with comb-over and sideburns gets out, closes gate.*

OC sound of fireworks continues.

MAN *in black overcoat with collar up, hat pulled down, appears suddenly.*

Driver looks around furtively, takes package from car and hands it to man who puts it inside his coat and quickly walks on.

SHEELAGH *(12) – a would-be sorceress – watches from undergrowth opposite graveyard. Her face is covered with sooty streaks.*

                    SHEELAGH
     KSSSSSSSSSSSS!

She hisses and spreads her fingers in direction of hearse as it drives away.

EXT. GARDEN – DAY

The Sun is disappearing. A firework bursts in the darkening sky.

REX *hears noise below, raises a rusty paint pot as if to pour.*

                    SHEELAGH (OC)
          It's Sheelagh from Number 15.

SHEELAGH *climbs swiftly and with remarkable skill towards tree-hut.*

She stops at entrance and holds up her open hand as if making a vow.

SHEELAGH

'By word, by deed, by good cheer'.

REX

Enter.

SHEELAGH

(Pointing at paint pot)
Is that wee?

REX

My grandmother's.

SHEELAGH

Potent.

REX

You're supposed to give the password before your ascent. What is your business?

SHEELAGH

I need you to climb into the church with me. And bring a saw.

REX

Has this been sanctioned by Lower Wood?

SHEELAGH

This is my operation.

REX

I'm busy. Lighting the bonfire in one hour. Get your own climbers…
(*with mocking voice*)
Paw-Drig – or Shay-Muss. Or better still – The Unpronounceable One.

SHEELAGH

Who?

REX

Jeer-Mud.

SHEELAGH

It's Deer-mwid. I need you, despite your
Saxon speech impediment. It's your church.

REX *swigs from a cordial bottle.*

REX

And you need a 'Black Protestant'?

SHEELAGH

Yes.

REX

Fancy that. Why should I help you? It's Halloween.
I have duties.

SHEELAGH

Halloween? Halloween? That's the feast of the
invader. This is Samhain.

SHEELAGH *holds up her hand, indicating a tiny gap between
her thumb and index finger.*

SHEELAGH

Tonight, that's all there is between this world and the
spirit world.
(*Exaggerating her pronunciation*) Samhain. Sow-in.

REX

You're boring me. This meeting is over.

SHEELAGH

Mr Deacon died.

REX

The old hunchback?

SHEELAGH

He's being buried tomorrow.

REX

Story goes he drowned a bag of kittens…

SHEELAGH

…and two of his children…

REX

…and two of his children… really?…in Priory Pond.

SHEELAGH

He's in the church overnight. And you're going to
help me climb in…

REX

Not a bother…

SHEELAGH

…and cut off his right hand.

REX *spits out a mouthful of cordial. He looks aghast.*

SHEELAGH

I need a murderer's right hand for my candle.
You can have one of the fingers – and a reputation
beyond compare.

REX *is trying to regain his composure.*

REX

I… I'd heard said you were practising spells.

REX *tries to make himself look busy.*

SHEELAGH

So, are you coming, Tree Lord?

REX

Er… no. Not really. Can't. Not practical, candles.
They blow out up here. You… need to leave. You only
gave the One Minute Password.

SHEELAGH *looks at him in surprise. She sneers.*

SHEELAGH

High Wood and Lower, and every tree between:
they all said you knew no fear. Now they'll know
differently. Halloween? God Save the Queen. Some
pink cushions up here would look nice.

REX *grabs his pot as if to drench* SHEELAGH.
*She smiles and makes childish 'Goodbye' gesture with her
hand before disappearing out of the door of the tree-hut and
climbing down.*
She is almost at the bottom of her climb.

REX (*OC*)

Two.

SHEELAGH *looks up.*
REX *is looking down from the tree-hut, his face now also
blackened with soot.*

REX

I want two fingers.

SHEELAGH

Very well.

REX

And the thumb.

SHEELAGH

Now you're pushing it.

REX *swings out on to the branches and descends, demon-
strating the same superb climbing skills as* SHEELAGH.
*Halfway down, his ragged pullover snags on a branch. He has
to reach back to release it.*

EXT. CHURCH ROAD – NIGHT
*The children walk quickly along the side of the quiet road that
leads to the church.*
REX *wears a small rucksack with a saw sticking out of it.*

They step back to conceal themselves as a car passes.
Up ahead is the church spire, black against the dark sky.
The horizon briefly whitens with the glow from exploding
fireworks.

REX
This is the weirdest, most dangerous, disgusting
thing I've ever been asked to do.

SHEELAGH
Wonderful though, isn't it?

REX's *face lights up.*

REX
Bloody marvellous.

EXT. GRAVEYARD – NIGHT
They hunker down between the graves near the church.

SHEELAGH
He's locked in there for the whole night. But let's be
quick, just in case.

SHEELAGH *goes to stand but* REX *pulls her back.*

REX
Wait. I know your heart is set on mastering sorcery.
That's understandable when you don't have your own
tree. But why do you want old Deacon's paw?

SHEELAGH
Ancient wisdom. A hand cut from a hanged
murderer, and burned in a candle made from fat
taken from his body is…

REX
Wait, wait. Fat? You'll want to make sausages out of
him next. I'm not scooping fat out: this is a 'hand-off-
and-away' job.

SHEELAGH

The hand will suffice.

REX

And who said he was hanged? How long do you think I've been up that tree for?

SHEELAGH

You badger me so. Regardless, when I light my candle, people nearby will become motionless, powerless to move.

REX

No surprise. It's going to smell utterly rank.

SHEELAGH

Enough chitchat.

SHEELAGH *stands.*

SHEELAGH

There will be a lot of interest in this prize. We don't want some evil force getting there before us, now do we?

EXT. CHURCH – NIGHT

SHEELAGH *and* REX *stand at the base of the tower, which is covered in thick, old ivy from the ground to the top.*
They look at one another, nod, and begin to climb the ivy effortlessly.
REX *leads.*
At a height of about thirty feet, SHEELAGH *stops suddenly.*

SHEELAGH

Hush up! Listen. Did you hear that?

REX

What?

OC a tearing sound. It gets louder.
REX *plunges past* SHEELAGH *as a swathe of ivy peels away*

from the wall.
REX *dangles precariously.*

SHEELAGH
Hold on! Hold on!.

REX *looks up wide-eyed, smiles, and lets go of the ivy.*
He holds his arms out, as if set to fly.
SHEELAGH *is horrified.*
He dangles, held by something.
Close on REX'*s snagged jumper.* REX *giggles nervously.*
OC a dog barks.

SHEELAGH
You dirty EEJIT! I thought you were gone.

REX
My lucky sweater!

Rex unhooks himself and climbs back up to Sheelagh, who
looks very unsure now.

SHEELAGH
I can't go on. I can't do it.

REX *climbs past her and looks back.*

REX
Sow-in. Fairies. Banshees. GIRLS. You'll never have
your own tree.

REX *reaches the battlement-style parapet of the bell tower.*

REX
At least come and keep lookout from the gallery
above the nave. I'll do the rest.

Bats burst noisily out of the belfry, startling REX.
He almost falls off parapet.
In the sky behind him, a rocket bursts into white spears.

INT. CHURCH – NIGHT

*The church is large with box pews on either side of a
central aisle.*

*REX walks slowly down the aisle, approaching the coffin in
front of the altar.*

*He looks back up at SHEELAGH, who watches anxiously from
the gallery above.*

*OC exploding rockets are frequent enough to sound like
thunder.*

*White flashes of light flood through the windows as if caused
by lightening.*

The carved skulls of memento mori look on.

REX

(*In stage whisper*)
I hope his eyes aren't bloody open. Just the right
hand, OK? No fat or anything like that. And I want
you to tell everyone. You tell them I did this on
my own.

He examines coffin.
The six screws securing the lid are topped by little crosses.

REX

You want to be a witch. But when the other Tree
Lords hear about this, they will declare me a GOD.

OC a louder explosion. SHEELAGH is startled.

SHEELAGH

Oh let's go. Let's get out of here. You know they'll kill
us if we're caught. And I do mean kill.

REX gets to work undoing the screws, which come out easily.
*Light alternates its entry into the church between stained-glass
and clear windows.*
The last screw comes out.
REX braces himself.
He lifts the lid off.

*The corpse is dressed in a dark suit, the arms and hands
concealed by the coffin's silk lining.*
REX *takes a deep breath, looks at* SHEELAGH *once more,
reaches in and lifts the right arm.*
REX *gasps.*
The hand is missing – the stump ragged.
The hand has been crudely hacked off.
OC two massive explosions in quick succession.
The windows rattle, the church interior is white.
REX *looks up at* SHEELAGH, *the mask of bravery slipping.*
REX *flings the handless arm back into the coffin.*
REX *spins around, away from the coffin, but something
holds him.*

REX

AAAAGH!

*He looks back to see the corpse is now sitting up, pulled to
that position by his pullover which is snagged on the dead
man's suit.*
He screams at the corpse.

REX

FLIP OFF!

REX *looks up to the gallery at a horrified* SHEELAGH.
Unseen by SHEELAGH, *a tall dark figure is standing directly
behind her.*
*OC another massive firework explodes nearby, drenching the
interior of the church in white light.*
For an instant, REX *can see who's standing behind*
SHEELAGH: *it's the driver of the hearse.*
The man is moving closer to SHEELAGH, *his expression grim.*
REX *pulls his sweater over his head, letting the corpse fall back
into the coffin.*

REX

LOOK BEHIND YOU!

JAMES MCDERMOTT

BEACHED

I'm trying to get ready for Auschwitz or school as I'm told
I should call it when suddenly
'Knock knock lover'.
Mum appears in my doorway.
'Can I have a word?'
'Have two: piss off.'
But in she trots, nearly trips over my Oscar Wilde books
then perches on my bed.
'Don't swear at me please thank you it spoils you. Look
lover. I'm worried'.
'What's that smell?'
'Ylang ylang. Radox. Don't change the subject. Look.
Before you hit sixteen, you were never in. Always out
gallivanting. But now… Your dad's cummerbund has more
outings than you. You are, you're reclusive.'
'Course I'm reclusive. I live in Sheringham. This place is a
prison. That's why I'm praying I've got good A Level results
so I can get out of this cesspit and get to the city where
there's music and people who are young and alive'.
Mum gives me her Anne Robinson eyes: she knows there's
something I'm not telling her. She's persistent. Like
Thatcher. The Iron Dinner Lady, that's what people call
her.
'Look. I'm fine all right? Happy as Larry.'
'I knew a Larry once. Killed himself. Might not've done if
he'd told his mum what were *really* wrong with him.'
I don't laugh cos I never laugh, no one laughs in
Sheringham, and cos I'm fighting the urge not to correct
her grammar: it's 'what was' wrong with him not 'what
were'.
Tina Turner, a girl in my history class, she always makes the
same mistake.
'Lover. We used to be thick as thieves. Now what's up?'
I look down at my Mister Men bed socks, stare at the little
hole in Mr Happy's chest, where his heart should be…
What's up? I'm sixteen. I'm gay. I live in Sheringham. I'm

fucked.

Well, I'm not actually, that's the problem. I've never even
been kissed.

Where can I explore round here? Rock pools?

Cos there's no gay scene in Sheringham. And I can't get
onto Grindr: shit 4G in Norfolk. The whole world's a gay
bar now but I can't get in.

Even if I could, everyone on Grindr just wants to, well,
come and go.

I just want someone to spoon, watch repeats of *Gogglebox*
with. *That's* what's up.

Course, I don't say any of that to Mum.

I could never tell her that I'm…

'I'm fine. Honest, Mum. Scout's honour.'

And I give the Scout's three finger-salute, like this.

I cycle to school along the seafront, plug myself into my
iPod: music will perk me up.

Shuffle: Queen's *I want to break free*.

Shuffle: Mousse T's *I'm horny*

Shuffle: The Beatles' *Eleanor Rigby*

Sheringham.

I pull up on the promenade and just look, out at the sea, out
at the world.

And I wonder if that's all I'll ever get to do: just look at it.

Oh when is my life going to start?

As I cycle past the Pearly Gates Retirement Home, I see
that someone's life is coming to an end: two paramedics are
carrying out a stretcher.

I run over to see if it's my old neighbour when a hand grabs
mine.

It's Brian, bad-breathed Brian, in his Crocs and corduroy
slacks.

'That's not Mrs M is it? On the stretcher?'

'Norris it is. On the stretcher. Seventy-four he was.

Good age.'
'Wasn't for Norris: he died. Is Mrs M in her room?'
'Sat in front of *Murder, She Wrote*. Tell her I'll be in with her
Maxwell House in a tick.'

I shout into Mrs M's good ear: 'Morning Mrs M. How you
keeping?'
'Knackered. Brian woke me up middle of the night cos he
forgot to gimme me sleeping pills. I couldn't get back off
after that. Spent rest of night staring at that poster they've
framed on me wall, 'love laugh live', ya seen it? Any road,
shush, I'm missing this. That Paki bastard who raped her,
telling ya.'
Mrs M makes Nigel Farage sound like Ghandi but she used
to buy me Capri Suns so I forgive her race hate.
Mrs M's sat in her overcoat. Her suitcase is packed by her
chair. As per, she says:
'Today's the day. Today's the day my man comes to take me
out this shithole.'
Oh how I wish a man would take me out this shithole…

I'm on a slow cycle to Sheringham, struggling up
Weybourne Hill when suddenly
PPPPFFF!
My bicycle punctures on a hillside desolate…
BEEP BEEP BEEP
I jump onto the roadside, get ready to give the Vs to the car
but it's stopped.
And the driver's getting out and…
Wait, is that…?
'Everything all right, Jimbo?'
Danny Doonan always asks the most ridiculous questions.
He's in my history set, puts his hand up the other day to ask
if Joan of Arc was Noah's wife.
A Level History's wasted on him.
He's got sales assistant written all over him. Spelt wrong,

cos of his dyslexia.

It's written just underneath 'prick' cos he's driving in sunglasses at nine in the morning.

He thinks he looks like James Dean. He does a bit, to be fair…

'Whack your bike in the boot if ya like? I'll give you a lift in the pussy wagon.'

He drives a Daewoo Matiz.

Michael Jackson's *Thriller*'s on in the car. *Human Nature*.

'This album right, this album, it's the greatest achievement of the twentieth century.'

'Oh really? I'll pass that on to Samuel Beckett.'

And Danny laughs without knowing why.

And suddenly… I'm laughing too.

I never laugh. No one laughs in Sheringham.

We stop at the traffic lights at the crossroads.

We're still laughing when he looks at me, locks eyes with me.

He's wearing Lynx Dark Temptation…

We stop smiling, *Thriller* stops too and then there's a silence.

A silence that grows louder and louder as we get closer and closer then…

The next song starts up.

MJ asks if we wanna be startin' somethin'.

MJ says we've gotta be startin' somethin'…

'I err, I can give ya a lift home later, if you like?

'Yeah yeah yeah no yeah I'd err… yeah I'd like that.'

My third smile in under a minute! What the fuck is going on?

The lights change to green and we're away…

And he does give me a lift home and he gives me a lift to school the morning after the morning after that and we start to spend break times lunch times night times together going for drives for chats and we both love Morrissey and we watch repeats of *Gogglebox* and we don't spoon but he looks at me like I'm the answer to something he makes me laugh sixty sometimes seventy times a day but I've stopped counting now cos it's becoming such a regular occurrence cos we're becoming really close. Friends.

Danny hasn't said he's not but if I mention girls or boys he changes the subject and…

He still loves the Scissor Sisters. Come on!

But he drives a pussy wagon doesn't he so?

I haven't told him that I'm…

But I've only really just told myself.

Perhaps it's time I said something…

We've pulled up by the darkened underpass on Sheringham Hill.

We're finishing off the kebab and chips we got from Jason's Donner Van.

Thriller's on again. Kinda growing on me now to be fair.

'Ah mate, this album right, it's – '

'The greatest achievement of the twentieth century?'

This gets us giggling and I see that Danny's got a bit of curry sauce on his chin so I scoop it off and suck my finger…

'Danny. There's err… there's something I want to say.'

'Yeah me too, mate.'

'What? You go first.'

The next song starts up: it's *Baby Be Mine*…

'Tina Turner. She's asked me out. Tina in our history class Tina not… yeah.'

'But… her grammar's appalling.'

'I'm thinking of saying yeah. Sorry.'

'What for?'

'Err, nothing. What did you wanna say to me?'

'Nothing'.

And I turn MJ off.

'Danny I'm… gonna walk home. I need the air, feel a bit groggy, probably the kebab.'

'What? No wait Jimmy mate look listen –'

But it's too late, I'm off down Sheringham Hill, plugging myself into my iPod, music will perk me up.

Shuffle: Will Young's *Jealousy*

Shuffle: The Beatles' *All You Need is Love*

Shuffle: *What's Love Got To Do With It?*

TINA TWATTING TURNER!

Love is pointless. Not that I was in love no way not with him as if shuddup.

Love's just another stupid thing stupid people do to fill time between the womb and the tomb and…

Shit: there's an ambulance outside the Pearly Gates.

Two paramedics running in with a stretcher, bad-breathed Brian running behind…

'She was watching *Bergerac*. Got up to go to the lav when she tripped over her suitcase. Smashed into the wall and that framed 'love laugh life' poster came crashing down, cracked her on the bonce.'

'Is she all right, is she breathing, do they think she'll be OK?'

Brian looks down at his Crocs…

And Mrs M's carried past.

And a tear snakes down onto my lip.

And I swear it tastes of Capri Sun.

I'm left alone in her room with that framed poster staring at me…

Love. Laugh. Live.

And in that moment… I vow I'll do just that. When I still can, wherever I am.

Beep beep.

Excuse me: phone…

'Danny – call incoming'…

Do I just tell him how I feel?

But what about Tina Turner?

Oh fuck Tina Turner, he loves the Scissor Sisters…
'Danny? What do you want?'
'You. I'm on Sheringham promenade. Can I see ya?'

He tastes like Polos, donner meat and curry sauce.
My first kiss! Yes!
Ooh it's clumsy at first: noses, chins, his shades getting in
the way, but he takes 'em off and we soon melt into it.
'I always knew Danny. Pussy wagon? The lady doth protest
too much. If we're to be a thing, you are losing the shades'.
'What? Why? People call this the James Dean look.'
'They mean his look *before* the crash.'
And we fall about laughing, we run down to the sea, there's
no one else on the beach, just me and him, alone and
immortal and we stand and we look.
Out at Sheringham.
Our own little bit of the world.

'Knock knock lover.'
I'm listening to *Thriller* when Mum appears in my doorway.
'Ya never off that phone.'
'I'm talking to Danny'.
'Who's Danny?
'Danny's… a friend. From school. A school friend from
school. Why all the questions, Juliet Bravo?'
'No no no I'm just, curious that's all… Are you? Curious?'
And I look down at my socks and…
And there's no hole anymore.
In Mr Happy's chest, where his heart should be; Mum
must've patched it up…
'Mum… I'm not like other boys.'
'Good. Other boys are crap.'
'No they're not. Or else why would I like 'em so much?'
And Mum, she trots over to me, nearly trips over my pile
of Oscar Wilde books, lifts up my chin, looks into my eyes,
sees everything I am and she says:

'I love the bones of you. And whatever, whoever you are…
whatever, whoever you… your bones will always be the
same. Ooh and you, you're gonna go so far lover, now
you've got those A Level results'.
'Yeah… I'm gonna defer for a year'.
'Ey? You were gonna escape, see the world?'
'I've only just started to see Sheringham. Rest of Norfolk to
see first. What's that smell?'
'Jojoba. Nivea.'
'I thought you only ever used Radox?'
'People change lover. Look. I don't mind you deferring… as
long as you're happy.'
'I'm happy as Larry. Scout's honour'.
And we give each other the scout's three-finger salute,
like this.

BIOGRAPHIES

KEITH BRADLEY is a former systems analyst and jockeys' agent who represented, among many others, the 2007 joint champion Seb Sanders. Originally from Manchester, he has lived in Newmarket for 24 years, where he is currently developing a horseracing sitcom and a play that is part family saga and part comment on the current housing crisis.

JONATHAN CROSS is a Film & Television Studies graduate (UEA; '15) and a current MA Scriptwriter. Born and raised in Leicestershire, and soon to be moving to London in the wildly optimistic hope of breaking into the film industry. He has made various short films.

SIMON FARNHAM delivers strong messages through the mouths of powerful characters. He has worked as a barrow boy, scaffolder, firefighter, bouncer, journalist and teacher. Spending the first twenty-nine years of his life in London before moving to Brighton and then Beijing, he currently exists in Sheffield.

ANDREAS HADJIVASSILIOU is a Norwich-based writer. His first feature length screenplay was a semi-finalist in the 2015 Shore Scripts competition, and in 2016 he won the Bafta Rocliffe TV Drama competition. He is currently working on his second feature length script.

ELEANOR HERZOG is in the process of completing an MA in Scriptwriting. She writes across film, stage, radio and television and has a background in television drama development and production.

PATRICK HUGHES is a Liverpool-based playwright. Since graduating from the University of Glasgow he has been longlisted for the Bruntwood Pize and has had his debut play *Northern Flight* performed in The Everyman Theatre's studio space. He is also the co-writer of BBC award-winning short film *Soundtrack*.

JOHN INGRAM was born and raised in Dublin. Following a stint in the post-production sector, he ran TV and video production businesses for many years before deciding to concentrate on writing for film and television.

JAMES MCDERMOTT is a Norfolk-based playwright and performer. His plays include *Beached* (Latitude, Southwark Playhouse), *Dogsbody* (Southwark Playhouse), and *Half A Person* (University Of East Anglia). *Half A Person* was shortlisted for Soho Theatre's Verity Bargate Award 2015. James's new one man show *Rubber Ring* opens at The Pleasance Islington this November. James is currently developing new work with The Garage Norwich, Hightide and Velvet Trumpet Comedy Theatre Company. Twitter: @jamesliammcd.

STEVE WATERS is a playwright whose plays include *Temple* (Donmar Warehouse, 2015), *The Contingency Plan* (The Bush, 2009); he also wrote *The Secret Life of Plays* (Nick Hern Books, 2010).

ACKNOWLEDGEMENTS

Thanks are due to the School of Literature, Drama and Creative Writing at UEA in partnership with Egg Box Publishing for making the UEA MA Creative Writing anthologies possible.

We'd also like to thank the following people:

Trezza Azzopardi, Tiffany Atkinson, Andrew Cowan, Giles Foden, Vesna Goldsworthy, Sarah Gooderson, Rachel Hore, Kathryn Hughes, Sarah Jones, Catrina Laskey, Timothy Lawrence, Jean McNeil, Jeremy Noel-Tod, Beatrice Poubeau, Denise Riley, Sophie Robinson, Kathy Scales, Helen Smith, Henry Sutton, Ian Thomson, Steve Waters, Peter Womack

Nathan Hamilton at Egg Box Publishing, Thom Swann and Ray O'Meara of A New Archive and Daniel Frost.

Editorial team:
Katherine Allen
Justine Ashford
Meghann Boltz
Sally Fox
Patrick Hughes
Rashmee Roshan Lall
Keely Celia Laufer
James McDermott
Lucy Malouf
Richard O'Halloran
Arron Westbrook
J Y Yang

COLOPHON

UEA Creative Writing MA Anthology:
Scriptwriting, 2016

International © 2016 retained by individual authors

A CIP record for this book is available from the
British Library.

Designed by A New Archive.

Cover illustration by Daniel Frost.

Proofread by Sarah Gooderson.

Printed and bound in the UK by TJ International.

Distributed by
NBN International,
10 Thornbury Road
Plymouth PL6 7PP
t. +44 (0)1752 2023102
e. cservs@nbninternational.com

ISBN: 978-1911343110